Sports Illustrated
POWERBOATING

The Sports Illustrated Library

BOOKS ON TEAM SPORTS

Baseball	Curling: Techniques and Strategy	Ice Hockey
Basketball	Football: Defense	Soccer
	Football: Offense	Volleyball

BOOKS ON INDIVIDUAL SPORTS

Badminton	Horseback Riding	Table Tennis
Fly Fishing	Skiing	Tennis
Golf	Squash	Track and Field: Running Events

BOOKS ON WATER SPORTS

Powerboating	Small Boat Sailing
Skin Diving and Snorkeling	Swimming and Diving

SPECIAL BOOKS

Dog Training	Training with Weights
Safe Driving	

Sports Illustrated
POWERBOATING

By TONY GIBBS

**Illustrations by
Russ Hoover**

J. B. LIPPINCOTT COMPANY
Philadelphia and New York

U.S. Library of Congress Cataloging in Publication Data

Gibbs, Tony.
  Sports illustrated powerboating.

  (The Sports illustrated library)
  1. Motor-boats.   I. Sports illustrated (Chicago).
II. Title.   III. Title: Powerboating.
GV835.G52   797.1'25   72-13277
ISBN-0-397-00971-2
ISBN-0-397-00972-0 (pbk.)

Copyright © 1973 by Time Inc.

Second Printing

Printed in the United States of America

Cover photograph: William Munro

Motor Boating & Sailing photographs on pages 10, 20, 30, 33, 39, 51, 52, 60, 61, 68, 78, 86 by Marta Norman and Pete Smyth

Contents

Author's Note

THERE ISN'T space in an introductory book like this to include information about handling every kind of motorboat on the water, so we've concentrated here upon the kind of small powerboat most commonly used in the United States today. Statistics suggest that your boat is probably 15 or 20 feet long, propelled by an outboard or sterndrive, and that it doesn't have a cabin.

Techniques for mastering a boat like this will serve you at the helm of bigger vessels, when you get around to them. No book can teach you everything there is to know about boating, and that's half the lure of the sport: there's always something new to try, no matter how good you become. Having finished this basic volume, you may want to continue your boating education through the nationally available courses offered by the U.S. Coast Guard Auxiliary and U.S. Power Squadrons. If you meet their qualifications for membership, you may choose to join one or both of these organizations and pass on what you've learned to others.

Whatever course you set for yourself, you'll find a tremendous satisfaction afloat once you absorb fully the basics of powerboat-handling skill and safety contained here.

Sports Illustrated
POWERBOATING

Choosing Your Boat

HULL TYPES AND CONSTRUCTION

TO KNOW a given motorboat, the first thing you must understand is her hull—the container in which passengers, gear and machinery are supported. Unlike cars or aircraft, boats operate in two very different mediums—air and water —at once. Since water is so much denser than air, it's water that both holds the boat up and at the same time slows her progress. So the most important part of a boat's hull is what's below the waterline.

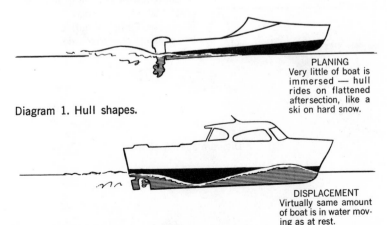

Diagram 1. Hull shapes.

PLANING
Very little of boat is immersed — hull rides on flattened after section, like a ski on hard snow.

DISPLACEMENT
Virtually same amount of boat is in water moving as at rest.

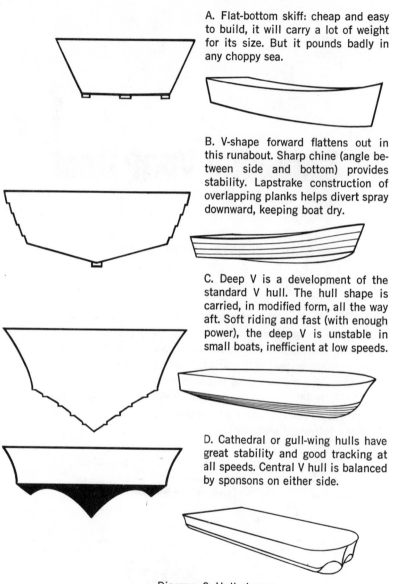

A. Flat-bottom skiff: cheap and easy to build, it will carry a lot of weight for its size. But it pounds badly in any choppy sea.

B. V-shape forward flattens out in this runabout. Sharp chine (angle between side and bottom) provides stability. Lapstrake construction of overlapping planks helps divert spray downward, keeping boat dry.

C. Deep V is a development of the standard V hull. The hull shape is carried, in modified form, all the way aft. Soft riding and fast (with enough power), the deep V is unstable in small boats, inefficient at low speeds.

D. Cathedral or gull-wing hulls have great stability and good tracking at all speeds. Central V hull is balanced by sponsons on either side.

Diagram 2. Hull shapes.

While any motorboat has to be designed to float herself and her contents, details of the hull shape are dictated by a number of other considerations: speed, for one; economy of construction is another; capacity is an important third; and performance, aside from sheer speed, can often be the fourth. Let's look at some hulls to see why they do what they do.

Material has a lot to do with shape, too. For instance, the kind of sheet plywood used in building inexpensive boats cannot assume a compound curve—that is, it will only bend in one direction at a time. Molded plywood can take any shape required, but the price can be high.

Far and away the most popular material for today's complex hull shapes is fiberglass, which should be called what it really is: fiberglass-reinforced plastic. The layers of coarse fiberglass strands (often woven into mat or cloth) are laid over or inside a mold, then thoroughly soaked with resin plastic in liquid form. When the resin is activated (usually by heat), it sets up hard in the boat's permanent shape.

As a building material, fiberglass is very strong but rather flexible. When its surfaces are curved, they reinforce themselves, adding a strength derived from shape to that of the basic material. What this means to you is that the complicated hull shapes—gull wing, cathedral and deep V—are not only cheap to build (being molded), but are also structurally extra strong.

Of all construction materials now in common use, only wood has inherent flotation. And as engines become larger and heavier, even an all-wood boat will be dragged to the bottom if she's swamped or punctured. Flotation tanks were pioneered in early aluminum runabouts, but these air-filled compartments would only function as long as they remained airtight. Today's boats usually derive their flotation from expanded plastic foam, much like what's used in life preservers. The foam can be sprayed into odd-shaped compartments, filling them completely, then sealed in place.

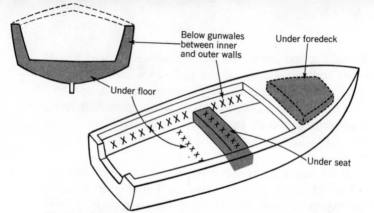

Diagram 3. Best flotation location is in gunwales or between double hulls high up: swamped boat will float upright. Boat with under-cockpit flotation won't sink, but it may float upside down.

Even if the compartment itself is holed, the hundreds of thousands of independent bubbles in the now-rigid foam will continue to support boat and crew.

ENGINE OPTIONS

Your boat and her engine should be a carefully considered team, not a haphazard combination. There are two power questions every new boat owner has to face: *how much?* and *what kind?* To answer the first, boating industry researchers have come up with the chart shown here, which

Diagram 4. To use graph, multiply length times beam of boat. Find equivalent figure (in feet) along left-hand column; directly below intersection of arc and length-beam product is number indicating maximum usable horsepower for boat.

HOW BIG SHOULD YOUR ENGINE BE?

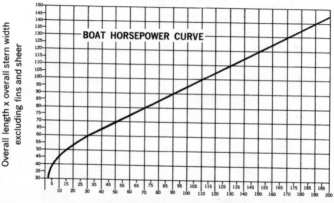

Overall length x overall stern width excluding fins and sheer

BOAT HORSEPOWER CURVE

MAXIMUM BOAT HORSEPOWER

Figure 1. Capacity plate for outboard gives maximum size of motor, proper load under average conditions. Number of seats is not an indicator of number of people boat can carry.

relates the average boat's length and beam (width) to the maximum engine horsepower that can be used safely and effectively. With no other information available, this graph will serve for the boat of normal shape, but most new boats come equipped with a capacity plate showing the maximum safe load as well as the largest motor for which the hull was designed.

What kind of engine? The standard inboard, contained inside the hull, is much like the engine in your family car. Instead of transmitting its power to an axle and thence to a pair of wheels, a marine engine turns a shaft that runs through a watertight gland called a stuffing box, then through the hull, to a propeller. Since the prop can only draw water from directly ahead and expel it astern to move the boat straight forward, a rudder is required to redirect the propeller's thrust and thus turn the boat.

Diagram 5. Inboard prop thrust.

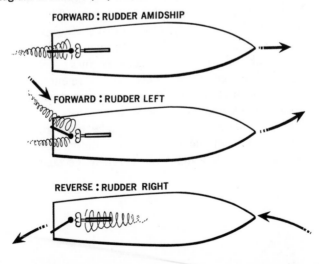

FORWARD : RUDDER AMIDSHIP

FORWARD : RUDDER LEFT

REVERSE : RUDDER RIGHT

It should be clear, too, that a boat (again unlike a car) pivots near the stern, since that's where the rudder is, rather than turning around the bow. And you can probably guess —accurately—that an inboard-powered boat won't steer very well in reverse.

Propeller, shaft and rudder are all vulnerable to damage from driftwood or grounding, and the necessary openings for propeller shaft and rudder stock are just two extra holes in the boat, and a frequent source of leaks.

Diagram 6. Inboard drive.

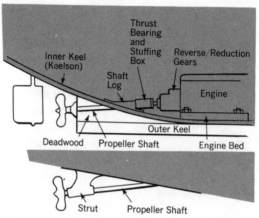

The obvious solution for small and medium-size boats is an outboard motor. Self-contained and removable, the outboard combines powerhead, vertical drive shaft, gearbox and propeller—and there are no holes through the hull. Only the fuel tank and (in electric-start engines) battery are separate. There's no rudder, since the entire motor pivots to change the direction of the propeller thrust: steering is precise, and as accurate in reverse as in forward.

When not in use, an outboard can be tilted to remove the lower unit from the water. If the leading part of the gearbox hits an underwater obstacle when the boat is mov-

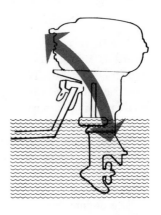

Diagram 7. Outboard drive.

ing forward, the engine will swing up automatically; special shock absorbers or sacrificial shear pins keep damage to a minimum.

All this may make an outboard seem too good to be true —and it does have some unavoidable drawbacks. An outboard sits on the very stern of the boat—the transom— and despite the engine's relatively light weight, there's still a heavy load right aft, as well as great stress on the transom itself. Outboards, even after much improvement, are far noisier than inboards, and the maximum practical size of the motor is about 150 horsepower. For fishermen, highpowered outboards have the additional problem of fouled sparkplugs when the engine is run at slow trolling speeds for any length of time—not to mention the line-snagging potential of the motor itself.

Diagram 8. Outboard prop thrust.

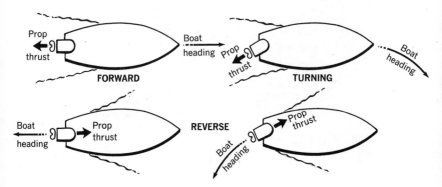

A relatively new compromise between inboard and outboard is the sterndrive, also known as outdrive, I/O and inboard-outboard. This unit is simply the marriage of inboard engine and outboard drive unit, with the actual drive shaft running through the transom slightly above the waterline. An outdrive's lower unit pivots and tilts just like an outboard's, and it provides the same steering and beaching advantages. To make tilting easier, most outdrives have a power mechanism to raise and lower the drive unit hydraulically.

The engine, usually a standard four-cycle marine inboard, offers an inboard's good operational economy and extra power. It must, of course, be mounted all the way aft against the transom, which creates some design problems, but the big difficulty with sterndrives to date has been the mechanical linkage between the engine and the drive unit: despite considerable improvement, this complex junction is still prone to breakdowns.

Nearly every engine manufacturer supplies controls—usually only a throttle and gearshift lever on the same mounting—for his make of outboard or I/O, but very few throttle-gearshift sets work exactly the same: sometimes the throttle lever is larger, sometimes it's the gearshift; one lever may, in certain installations, handle both functions.

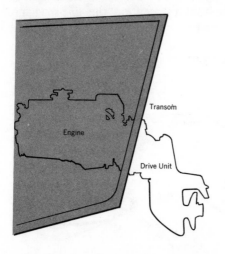

Diagram 9.
Inboard-outboard drive.

There are a couple of things to remember that apply to all marine controls. First, learn (from the owner's manual) the engine speed range in which you can shift gears without damaging them. (Most outboards have built-in stops that do this for you.) Second, when taking charge of an unfamiliar boat, be certain you know which is throttle, which gearshift. Third, because of propeller slippage in water, a little added throttle may be necessary to get the boat moving—but the first burst of power in a single-engine boat will usually throw the bow slightly to the left before she begins to move forward. Finally, bear in mind that reverse in a boat is the same as a brake in your car, but you should never expect to slam a boat from fast forward to full astern. If you do, the stern will probably slue wildly from side to side, and an outboard engine may well leap clear of the water: slow the boat down off planing speed, *then* put her in neutral till she is just under control in forward, *then* apply reverse.

To familiarize yourself with a boat's controls, take her out in an open harbor, away from traffic, and learn how she handles. Find out how much throttle it takes to get your boat moving, what additional throttle is necessary to get her onto a plane. See how long it takes to decelerate from quarter throttle, half throttle and full throttle. Try tight turns at varying speeds. Practice maneuvering forward, then backward at slow speeds. In short, get the feel of your craft. This brief familiarization run will help a great deal when you later have to maneuver in congested harbors.

2
Safety Rules

IF YOUR boat breaks down while you're out on the water, you usually can't walk home, so it's a good idea to take a few more precautions before you go than you might before driving off in your car.

1. Never leave the dock without telling some reliable person ashore where you plan to go and when you expect to return. That way, if something goes wrong, searchers will know when and where to start looking.

2. If you're planning a long trip, leave an itinerary, so people will know what route you took.

3. Keep near your home phone a complete description of your boat (see Chapter 8): you might be surprised how easily worried people can forget details like length, registration numbers or the exact color of the topsides.

4. Check the weather before you leave your house: most area weather bureaus have a recorded forecast for telephone callers; if you rely on radio, make sure it's a *marine* forecast you're listening to. (During the boating season, most

stations in shoreside communities give marine forecasts in the morning and early evening.)

At the pier, there's another set of things to check off:

1. Is your boat in condition to go, with all necessary gear aboard and working?

2. Are your fuel tanks—main and reserve—topped up?

3. When the engine's started, do the gauges (for battery, oil pressure and water pressure) read normal?

LOADING YOUR BOAT

Loading a small boat properly is sometimes more tricky than it looks. Major weights—people, fuel, batteries—have a proportionally greater effect on the boat's balance than they do in larger vessels. Most small powerboats don't heel easily at first, nor does extra weight make them ride obviously low in the water—but today's powerboats operate at a high level of performance, which means that a relatively slight heel or a little overload can affect the boat's handling very much.

When leaving a pier or making a landing, everyone aboard who's not actually working the boat should sit down. Keep

Diagram 10. Concentrate weights low down and in center of boat; this minimizes unexpected tipping.

hands and feet inboard when anywhere near a dock or other boat, and don't allow passengers to ride on the unprotected foredeck of a small motorboat: not only does this make the boat nose-heavy and hard to steer; it also invites fatal accidents.

Nonswimmers in the boat should wear life preservers. It's sometimes hard to make passengers put on a life jacket, but there are reasonably comfortable preservers now on the market, so the old argument about bulkiness doesn't really apply any more. Remember: if it's your boat or if you're acting as skipper, the life of everyone aboard is your responsibility, both morally and legally.

GASOLINE—DANGERS

Gasoline has to be highly combustible to do its job inside your engine. Unfortunately, it's highly explosive elsewhere as well. In liquid form, gasoline will burn fiercely; when gasoline becomes a vapor mixed with air, it then has the capacity to blow you into the middle of next week: a teaspoon of fuel, once vaporized, has the potential force of three sticks of dynamite. And it's invisible.

Gasoline vapor is heavier than air, so it will sink to the lowest point in the boat and collect there. A car, by contrast, has no airtight structure, so spilled fumes just drop down to the pavement where the breeze dissipates them. When gassing up, make sure you take the following steps:

1. If you have portable tanks, remove them from the boat and fill up at the gas pump. Wipe off spills before replacing them and strapping them down in the boat.

2. Before filling installed tanks, make sure no one is smoking and that all flames are out and electrical circuits closed.

3. Shut all ports and hatches, to keep fumes out of the boat's interior.

23

Diagram 11. Grounding the hose nozzle while fueling.

4. When running gas, keep the hose nozzle touching the rim of the tank or fill pipe to prevent the buildup of static electricity.

5. After fueling, seal the tank and hose off all spilled fuel. (But try to avoid spilling gas in the first place: petroleum products are among the most harmful substances to birds and marine life generally.)

6. Open hatches and ports, start the bilge blower, and air the boat out for five minutes. Before starting the engine, sniff the bilge for gas fumes: if they're present in dangerous concentration, you'll smell them.

Boats with enclosed engine or fuel-tank spaces must have installed ventilation according to the diagram shown here. If you're in doubt whether your boat is legally rigged, get in touch with your local Coast Guard Auxiliary unit and ask for a free Courtesy Motorboat Examination (see Chapter 8).

Diagram 12. (Opposite)
Basis of proper ventilation is one vent in, one out, for each engine of fuel compartment. Vent tubing should be flexible and wire-reinforced. Intake vent leads at least halfway down; exhaust vent draws air from lowest point in compartment. Minimum practical diameter of vent tubing is 3 inches; ventilators should be trimmed so as to face properly when boat is under way. A mechanical blower is the most effective way to exhaust any compartment, but its motor must be spark-proof.

24

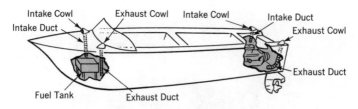

INBOARD-OUTBOARD STERN DRIVE
Separate Fuel Tank and Engine Compartments

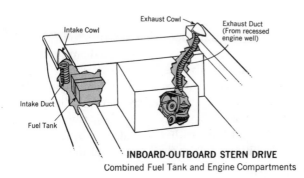

INBOARD-OUTBOARD STERN DRIVE
Combined Fuel Tank and Engine Compartments

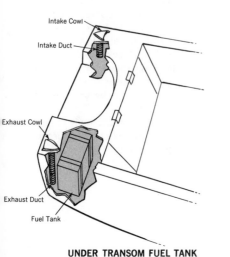

**UNDER TRANSOM FUEL TANK
COMPARTMENT (Outboard)**

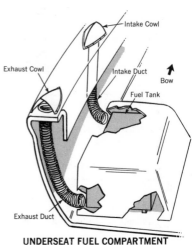

UNDERSEAT FUEL COMPARTMENT

Figure 2. Planing.

SPEEDS

Your boat's designed operating speed is probably about two-thirds throttle, for a standard runabout with engine matched to hull. At this speed, your boat should be planing mostly on the water's surface and in a relatively horizontal position. If this isn't the case, try moving the passengers about. If the boat still squats or mushes, you may be able to adjust her attitude with trim tabs or by changing the angle of the outboard drive shaft relative to the hull.

Incorrect—bow high.

Correct by angling prop forward.

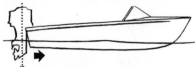

Incorrect—bow down.

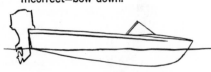

Correct by angling prop aft.

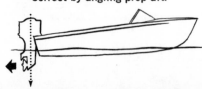

Diagram 13. Boat down by the stern has trouble planing, throws huge wave, pounds badly. If the bow is very high, it will be blown from side to side. Bow-heavy craft pushes a lot of extra water, tends to steer erratically, may be very wet in choppy sea.

Change in shaft angle of outboard or I/O changes thrust of propeller, driving bow down or up, as required.

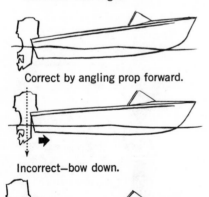

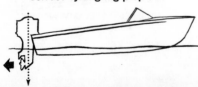

RULES OF THE ROAD

Once you are clear of piers and docks, your problems as skipper will usually come from other boats. Because water-craft aren't restricted to visible roadways, there's a fairly complex body of regulations—the Rules of the Road—which governs any boat's actions when in the presence of other vessels. In the United States, as it happens, there are four different sets of Rules of the Road in force. Which one applies to you depends on where you do your boating.

International Rules have effect not only on the high seas but also along our coasts. Dovetailing in jurisdiction are the Inland Rules, which cover boats in bays, harbors and inlets connecting to the sea, such as Chesapeake Bay, Long Island Sound, San Francisco Bay. There's a third group of rules for Great Lakes boatmen and a fourth for skippers operating on Western rivers, which is generally taken to mean the Mississippi system plus a few others, but not rivers on the Pacific Coast.

Most boatmen have to learn only a single group of rules, but those who keep their craft in waters where two juris-dictions come together will have to keep two sets separate in their minds. For instance, the Miami sailor will observe Inland Rules as long as he's in Biscayne Bay, but once he ventures outside into the Atlantic, he must govern his boat according to the International Rules.

All Rules of the Road have a single objective: *preventing collision.* The different groups of rules are largely—*but not entirely*—similar to each other. Each set of rules has two parts—the headings dealing with identifying lights and shapes carried by ships and boats (see Chapter 4), and the steering and sailing rules, considered here.

The whole system of Rules of the Road rests on two words, "privileged" and "burdened." When there is danger of collision between two vessels, one is usually privileged,

27

RULES OF THE ROAD

Situation	Who privileged	Action taken	Horn signal
MEETING	Neither vessel *	Each skipper should swing right, then straighten out to pass port side to port side.**	1 blast of horn ***
CROSSING	Boat on right of other boat ##	Privileged vessel sounds 1 blast, maintains course and speed; burdened answers, takes necessary avoiding action.#	1 blast by each
OVERTAKING	Boat overtaken	Burdened (overtaking) boat swings left, clears privileged boat's wake, then passes on privileged's port side. Passing boat remains burdened until he is clear ahead.	2 blasts by overtaking boat, if he wishes to pass on privileged's port; 1 blast to overtake to starboard. Privileged gives same signal in response if he agrees ****

* Under Great Lakes Rules, vessel going downstream in a river is privileged. On Western Rivers, boat going upstream gives whistle signal indicating preferred passing side.

** Boats can also pass starboard to starboard, but better course of action is to pass as cars do—left side to left side.

*** Generally speaking, 1 blast means, "I am changing course to my right"; 2 blasts mean, "I am changing course to my left"; 3 indicate, "My engines are in reverse"; 4 or more mean danger, or, "I do not agree with what your signal proposes."

**** If privileged or burdened skipper disagrees with any signal, he must give the danger signal. This is the **only** signal to give if you feel the other boat is proposing or actually doing something that will put one or both of your vessels in danger.

Under International Rule, no sound signal is given.

To determine if crossing situation exists, learn to recognize your boat's **danger zone:** the arc from dead ahead to 2 points aft of the starboard beam, or just about equal to your field of vision from straight ahead as far right as your eyes can see without moving your head. Any boat in this danger zone is crossing and is privileged with respect to your boat, unless she's coming right at you from ahead.

Diagram 14. Rules of the road.

the other burdened: these are technical terms and don't mean what they do in ordinary conversation. A privileged vessel is one which is required by the rule to maintain her course and speed as closely as possible; a burdened vessel has the corresponding duty to avoid the privileged vessel the best way her skipper can manage: he can continue on course, if he thinks that's safe, or he can stop, change course, even reverse. It's up to the burdened skipper, but he has the responsibility for whatever he decides to do.

Privileged and burdened aside, every skipper is expected to use his head: if there is no way to avoid collision under the rules, then any action taken to prevent the boats' colliding is justified.

Under most rules, two types of vessels are specially privileged with respect to ordinary powerboats: commercial fishing boats towing nets or trawls (but not trolling lines) are entitled to maintain course and speed over all other vessels; and sailboats under sail alone are privileged over power vessels *except* fishermen, large vessels in narrow channels, and powerboats which the sailboat is overtaking.

When fog closes in, sound signals are prescribed by law for all vessels, whether under way or at anchor. If fog is forecast, your best move is to stay in the harbor; but if you should be caught out, remember that the fog will usually lift in a few hours at most.

FOG SIGNALS

	Inland	International	Great Lakes	Western rivers
POWER UNDER WAY	1 blast per minute	1 blast every 2 minutes	3 blasts each minute	2 short blasts and 1 long
BOAT TOWING ANOTHER VESSEL	1 long, 2 short blasts	1 long, 2 short blasts	1 long, 2 short blasts, but vessel being towed rings a bell as well	3 evenly spaced blasts

Diagram 15. Fog signals.

29

The Rules of the Road aren't hard to live with, once you become familiar with them. But beware the other guy: never count on a boat behaving predictably unless you know the man or woman at the wheel. If you take early steps to avoid situations which might lead to collision, then you'll save yourself the worry of wondering if the other skipper is as knowledgeable as you are.

3
Handling Your Boat

WHILE NEARLY anyone can handle a modern motorboat reasonably well, it takes a real expert to get the most out of the vessel.

OPERATING IN ROUGH WEATHER

Handling any small craft in rough seas is largely a matter of making sure that the waves' force is neutralized as much as possible. A wave has tremendous power, and even a small one can seriously damage a ship *if* the sea strikes hull or superstructure flat on.

A beginning boatman should, of course, avoid being out in rough water in the first place: know your own ability and that of your boat, and if the state of the sea looks dangerous to you, don't let someone else talk you into leaving the pier. The government's storm-warning system will also give reliable guidance of coming trouble: learn

31

where the nearest weather-warning display station (usually at a yacht club, Coast Guard base, or large marina) is located; if a Small Craft or other storm warning is hoisted (see Chapter 8), stay ashore or in sheltered water. Remember that the weather warning may indicate a coming trend, so the water in your area can still be calm at the time a signal is hoisted. But be assured that any government weather-warning signal means serious bad weather on the way.

If you're caught out in rough seas, don't panic. Chances are your boat can absorb more punishment than you'd think—and probably more than you can. Nearly any boat is designed to take the waves best bow-on. Conversely, a boat's stern is frequently a vulnerable point: a breaking wave can run up over the transom, fill the cockpit, and even flood the engine. So when the boat begins to roll uncomfortably, try to head into the seas, at an angle of 15 or 20 degrees to either side of the wave direction. This will allow the boat to sidle over the waves much the way a high jumper goes over a bar, and it'll probably be easiest on both boat and crew.

Even cathedral-hulled craft can be unhappy running broadside to the waves and a round-bottom skiff can roll in a sickening (literally) manner. Boats roll in a definite rhythm, and with each cycle the roll becomes more pronounced. If you see this pattern starting, break out of it by changing direction for a minute or two—and when changing direction in rough water, wait until a set of large waves has gone past and relatively smaller ones arrive, then swing the boat.

If you must run with the seas, try to ride the backs of large waves: with practice, a skipper can hold a maneuverable runabout on the back of the same swell for minutes at a time. Just don't get carried away and start riding the forward side of the wave: your boat may break out of control, swing sideways to the wave and roll over.

32

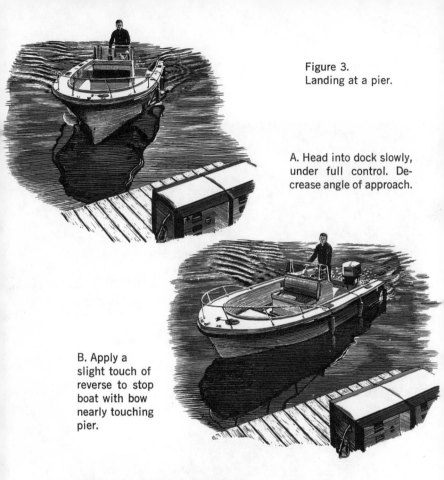

Figure 3.
Landing at a pier.

A. Head into dock slowly, under full control. Decrease angle of approach.

B. Apply a slight touch of reverse to stop boat with bow nearly touching pier.

APPROACHING A MOORING

While most motorboats are kept at piers or floats, every skipper should know how to approach a mooring—or any other floating object. Head the boat into wind and current (or if they're in opposition, against whichever is stronger), and slow down to your minimum speed while still retaining maneuverability. A crewmember should stand by with the boathook to snag the mooring, and should sing out when he's got it. If you miss on your first try, swing out and try the whole thing from the beginning—don't try to retrieve a bad pass in the middle.

LANDING AT AND LEAVING A PIER

Landing at a pier is trickier, since you have to take wind and current as they come: there's seldom more than one side at which you can berth. Before beginning your approach, plan which side you'll dock on, put out fenders (never count on dock padding), and get lines ready fore and aft. The accompanying illustrations show how the more common approaches are made—other situations are only variants of these.

C. Turn wheel all the way toward pier and apply a final touch of reverse to pull boat's stern in.

D. You should now be parallel to pier, close enough to step ashore.

Figure 4. Backing into a pier.

A. Backing into slip, bring boat at right angles to slip opening. Turn sharply away from shore.

B. While boat is still swinging out, put engine in reverse.

C. Now use reverse to pull boat backward into slip.

D. Remember that when going astern, boat pivots near the transom, following the engine.

E. Straighten out engine. Back straight in, parallel to and near side-finger of pier. Stop with a touch of forward.

Figure 4. (Continued)

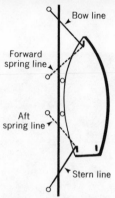

Bow line

Forward
spring line

Aft
spring line

Stern line

Diagram 16A. Tying up. Lines from the bow forward to a dock cleat, and from stern aft, are usually enough for a small boat. If you're going to leave the boat overnight, extra spring line—one from the bow cleat aft, the other from the stern forward—can be added.

You'll find that all these close-quarters evolutions become easy with practice; it's a good idea, when you first get a boat, to find a deserted pier and spend a couple of hours approaching it from every possible angle, till you know how to handle any kind of landing. You'll also learn where to hang out the fenders for each approach. And, finally, spend the extra few dollars required to get good, oversize fenders and a king-size boathook (for small boats, telescoping aluminum hooks that give you a choice of lengths from 4 to 8 feet are available).

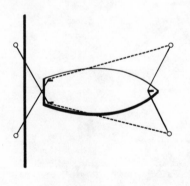

Diagram 16B. Dotted lines indicate dock lines used only if boat is as long as or longer than the slip.

40

Leaving a pier or slip is simple enough, unless you're pinned to the float by a strong wind or current. In a conventionally shaped boat, run a line from the bow to a cleat ashore located about amidships. Put the engine in slow forward; turn the wheel toward the dock. The curve of the boat's bow will cause the vessel to angle in forward, levering the stern away from the pier. When you're at the best possible angle, put the engine in reverse, straighten out the wheel, cast off quickly, and back out. Before you attempt this maneuver, which is called springing the boat, make sure you've got a nice, fat fender between the bow and the pier.

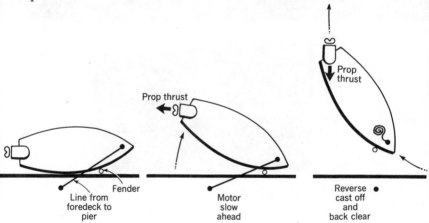

Diagram 17. Springing.

KNOT TYING AND LINES

The knots a skipper really needs to know are very few. For starters, get the few essential knots down right—so you can tie each one without looking at it. Then you can attempt more fancy ropework for the fun of it.

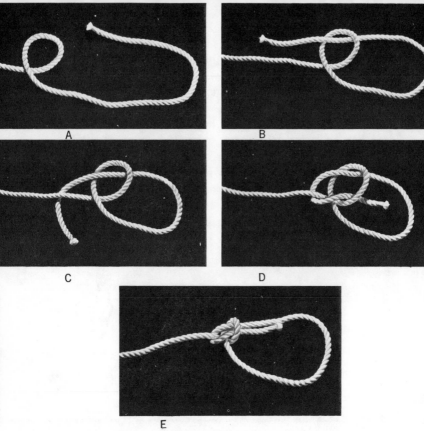

Figure 5. Tying a bowline.

Loop: for attaching a line to a piling or an anchor, the best loop is the familiar sailors' knot called a bowline (pronounced bō'-lin). If you use it to secure an anchor, double the loop.

Connecting two lines: if you can tie a square knot, it will serve well enough—*if* the lines you're connecting are the same size. If you can't tie a square knot without having it come out a granny half the time, then forget it and learn this one—called a sheet bend—instead: it's easy to tie, easy to untie; and it can be used for ropes of any size.

Figure 6. Sheet bend.

Line around a cleat: the idea is to make sure the initial stress is taken by the first turn—around the base of the cleat. A figure eight around the horn, finishing with a half hitch as shown, will enable you to untie the line without taking too much strain as you do so.

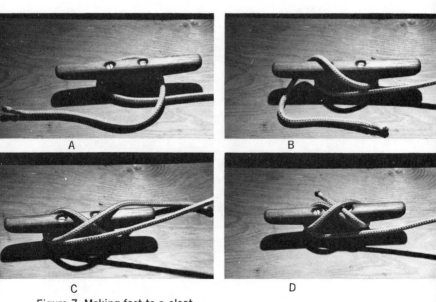

A

B

C

D

Figure 7. Making fast to a cleat.

There are three kinds of line commonly used aboard today's motorboats: manila is a natural fiber, relatively cheap and moderately strong; unfortunately, manila has a tendency to rot, so if you have a choice, steer clear of it and get nylon instead. Nylon is very strong and it doesn't rot; it also has tremendous stretch, which makes it ideal for anchor and dock lines, since the line itself can cushion the shock of waves against the boat. Finally, you may want to use polypropylene line where you need a rope that floats —as for waterski towlines or mooring pickups. Polypropylene is slippery and less strong than nylon, so it's not a good material for anchor or dock lines.

Nylon line suffers from prolonged exposure to sunlight, becoming brittle and lifeless. So unless your line is serving some purpose, stow it in a locker. Before doing so, make it up into a neat coil, as shown, so you won't have an unmanageable tangle when you open the locker next time.

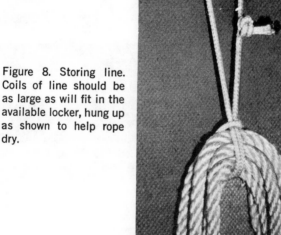

Figure 8. Storing line. Coils of line should be as large as will fit in the available locker, hung up as shown to help rope dry.

A.   B.

Figure 9. Anchors
A. Danforth anchor, 6 feet of chain, eye-spliced line make a good ground-tackle combination.
B. Plow anchor is another effective lightweight type.

ANCHORS AND ANCHORING

Though an anchor looks simple, it's actually the result of a good deal of sophisticated engineering. To get the most from any anchor, you have to know how to use it properly. An anchor works best when its shank is nearly parallel to the bottom, which means a long anchor line. For normal anchoring, when someone will be on or near the boat, a proportion of five lengths of anchor line to each length of water depth (referred to as a *scope of 5 to 1*) is adequate. But in bad weather or when the boat will be unattended for some time, a scope of 10 to 1 is better.

Weight has a good deal to do with an anchor's effectiveness. The accompanying table shows generally agreed-upon anchor weights for standard small powerboats. You can increase any anchor's holding power by inserting an 8-foot length of chain between the anchor and anchor line: this extra weight will hold the anchor's shank at a flatter angle, making the flukes penetrate better. A boat of any size at all should carry two anchors—a light one for everyday, a heavier one for rough weather.

45

When anchoring, bring the boat into wind or current and throw the engine out of gear. As the boat stops and begins to move backward, lower the anchor slowly over the bow and pay out line till you feel the anchor hit bottom. Now put the boat into reverse, continuing to feed out anchor line, until you've reached a scope of about 5 to 1. Take a turn around the bow cleat and continue reversing until the anchor sets and the boat won't move backward any more. If the anchor doesn't bite in and set, haul it in: the line may be tangled around the anchor itself, or the flukes may be jammed with seaweed or stones.

Anchor Weights. Proper anchor weights vary widely with individual designs, but the table below should be a guide for lightweight-type anchors—Danforth, Northill, Plow, etc.

Boat		Storm	Working
Length, ft.	Beam, ft.	anchor, lb.	anchor, lb.
10	4	8–10	4–6
15	5	8–12	5–8
20	7	10–15	5–12
25	8	12–25	8–12

(In the table above, first weight in each column is for a lightweight, low-profile boat of a given size; second figure for a higher, heavier craft.)

Yachtsman's or Herreshoff anchors are generally calculated to hold less well than modern, lightweight anchors. Some authorities give, as a rule of thumb, a weight of 1 pound per foot of boat length for a working yachtsman's anchor, 1½ pounds for a storm anchor.

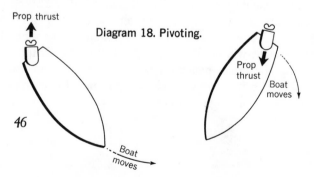

Prop thrust

Diagram 18. Pivoting.

Prop thrust

Boat moves

Boat moves

46

MANEUVERING

Maneuvering a boat in tight spaces isn't difficult, especially if you've mastered the techniques of landing described earlier. Perhaps the most dangerous boathandling areas are marinas, because of the high concentration of boats and the difficult visibility.

When coming out of a narrow row of slips, give a blast of your horn before you emerge. Conversely, if another skipper blows his horn from around a blind corner, wait till you can see his boat before you make a move. Many inboard boats turn more sharply in one direction than the other because of the propeller thrust; this isn't a problem with outboards or sterndrive boats, but such craft do have a tendency to turn more easily away from the wind than into it, because of the high bow and concentration of weight aft. Skippers of inboards generally dock their boats in slips stern first, as it makes boarding easier, but outboards and sterndrives present a fragile lower unit to the bulkhead in this position, so it's often wiser to park bow in—especially since an outboard or sterndrive has excellent maneuverability going astern.

SAFETY PRECAUTIONS

When in a narrow, crowded channel, be ready for anything: swimmers, waterskiers popping out from behind anchored boats, laden dinghies. Always keep clear of anything in the water unless you plan to pick it up or make fast

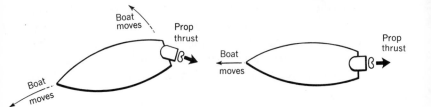

to it: like icebergs, most rubbish floats with more mass below the surface than above.

Stay clear of fishermen, too—not only commercial fishing craft, which have the right of way when fishing, but also boats trolling lines and fishermen on the beach. The nylon line used by most anglers can easily wrap itself around your prop; worse, it can saw right through the seals between propeller and gearcase, causing costly damage.

Large vessels, even when anchored, are another source of trouble. You may be swept against them by the current or you may suddenly discover that their huge props are still turning, throwing a dangerous screw current aft. Finally, stay well away from dams and weirs. This should be so obvious as to require no warning, but the lip of a dam may be nearly invisible from a low-lying boat, and every year many small-boat skippers have serious—often fatal—accidents with dam outflows.

This book isn't a text in fishing or waterskiing, but you as a skipper should know a few safety tips about each sport.

Waterskiing. Never have the engine in gear when near a man in the water; never have the engine running—even in neutral—when someone's getting aboard. Always have at least one other person in the boat, to act as spotter. Make sure someone's tending the towline whenever you're not actually under way with a skier. When passing a line to a skier in the water toss the rope just in front of him, then pull it into his grasp by swinging the boat. When under way, stay clear of the towline cleat or ring: if the line should snap, it'll come back at you like a whip, and anyone standing near could be badly injured.

Fishing. When trolling lines, govern your maneuvers—especially turns—accordingly. Don't troll near swimmers, among fleets of racing sailboats, or other fishermen; when someone hooks a fish, have the other anglers reel in if it's a big one. When casting (which should be done *only* with the boat at rest), space the fishermen so they don't hook

A – Faster

B – Speed O.K.

C – Left turn

D – Cut motor

E – Skier O.K. after fall

F – Slower

G – Right turn

H – Back to drop-off area

I – Stop

J – Pick me up
or fallen skier — watch out

Figure 10. Waterski hand signals.

When making a tight turn from a standing start, it's usually a good idea to put the wheel hard over, **then** give a quick burst of power in forward. If you can't complete the turn, put the engine in neutral, turn the wheel hard the other way, **then** give a burst of power in reverse: when the gears are engaged and the wheel hard over, a sudden thrust of acceleration will cause the boat to spin before she begins to move ahead, and she'll turn around a point somewhere aft of amidships—unlike a car. One thing to beware of is the swing of the stern in narrow places: beginning skippers often forget where the boat pivots and do a lot of damage just clearing the slip.

49

each other. Don't allow standing up to cast unless yours is a stable boat. Be especially alert for hooks and lures left lying about on seats or the floorboards: anybody who changes lures should put the old one away before tying on the new one.

If someone does get hooked, don't try to extract the hook alone. Clip off the lure, tape the hook in place on the victim, and head home for professional help.

4

Basic Navigation

CELESTIAL, or high-seas, navigation is both an art and a science. It can take years to master, but the kind of point-to-point coastal navigation (sometimes termed piloting) used by the inshore skipper is fairly simple and depends on knowledge of only a few navigational tools.

CHARTS

Most important of these is the nautical chart, a map that emphasizes shore and water features instead of land. Like any map, a chart is a picture of the earth's surface drawn to scale, and because a chart represents a large area of real ground or water, important objects can't be represented by scale drawings, which would be too small to see. Instead, landmarks and aids to navigation appear as symbolic shapes which don't pretend to look like the real things, but which are recognizable because they conform to an agreed-upon code.

It's been said that a land map shows you where you can go, while a chart shows where you can't: for small boats at least, most of the water's surface is "road," and only a few danger points are marked with buoys or other man-made aids to warn off the boatman. Larger vessels have to travel inside of nautical roads called channels, which are marked on either side (and sometimes along the center) by anchored buoys. In many cases the channel isn't man-made and simply conforms to the line of greatest depths.

BUOYS

The accompanying illustration shows the pattern of buoys used to mark the sides, center and obstructions in a typical channel. Buoys are numbered consecutively from a major body of water to a minor one, or going upstream on a river, or moving inland from the sea. Proceeding in this direction, red-painted buoys mark the right-hand side of the channel, black buoys the left. Many skippers find it easy to memorize the catchphrase "red-right-returning from the sea" to help fix this arrangement in mind. Red buoys are always even-numbered, black buoys are always odd-numbered. Unlighted red buoys, which look like upside-down cones, are called *nuns*, while unlighted black buoys look like what they're called: *cans*.

Lighted buoys of either color have no fixed shape, though they're usually grillwork towers with the light at the top. Red buoys show a red or a white light, while black buoys display a green or a white light.

Some buoys or markers are placed in the center of a channel: those striped vertically in black and white indicate the safe center of a straight channel; red-and-black horizontally striped buoys mark obstructions in the channel or a place where the channel forks.

A. Can.

B. Nun.

C. Lighted gong.

D. Red flasher.

E. Speed limit.

F. Spindle.

G. Lighthouse and bell.

Figure 11. Buoy shapes.

LANDMARKS

A chart showing your body of water isn't any good to you unless you can fix your own position on it—and that's the first step in any navigation. If you can see two or three buoys or charted landmarks, you should have no trouble calculating where you are, but a single buoy won't tell you too much, unless you're right next to it.

Landmarks, such as bridges and buildings, can be tricky to use, as many of them aren't noted on the chart at all: the government keeps charts updated with respect to buoys and other aids to navigation, such as lighthouses, but frequently a new building may not be added to the chart for years. Bridges are usually reliable landmarks to use, as they're not built too frequently and their towers are often visible for miles. Odd structures, such as those in a shoreside amusement park, can also be very helpful.

DEPTHS

Depths on most charts are marked in feet, but on charts of tidal waters, the depth shown is usually that of the water at the lowest normal low tide. In a box on the chart you'll find the range of tide—the difference between high and low water. After a while you'll learn to note subconsciously the state of the tide and bear it in mind, as well as whether the tide is rising or falling. In most cases, however, the depth figures on the chart indicate a safe amount of water that you can count on.

LIGHTS

At night, when only lights are visible, the average bay or lake looks entirely different, and it's easy for a novice boatman to get completely lost. But if you can recognize the standard lights of other boats and of charted aids to navigation, you should have no trouble finding your way.

There are three kinds of lights you'll see at night on the water: random lights from ashore or from the cabins of boats; running and anchor lights of vessels, which tell you how big and what type a boat is; and lights on aids to navigation, which tell by their color and pattern of blinking what the marker is.

A boat's running lights are designed to show others where and what she is; they aren't meant to help a skipper see where he's going. When you know what to look for, you can tell by looking at another vessel's lights what general size she is, if she is a special-purpose craft (like a ferry or a police boat), what direction she's going, and whether she or your boat has the right of way. The accompanying chart of running lights shows the patterns you're most likely to see on the water, but there isn't room here to illustrate all the variations that apply to special-purpose vessels.

In addition, far too many boatmen display incorrect running lights, either out of ignorance or because the electrical system isn't working properly: even though you know what you're doing at night, you can bet that a good percentage of the other people on the water don't.

While nearly all lights on boats are fixed—that is, they shine unblinkingly—lights on aids to navigation usually flash on and off in a preset pattern which is noted on the chart, right alongside the symbol for the particular aid or buoy, in abbreviated form. Learn the standard abbreviations (there aren't many). Bear in mind, too, that lights are not all the same strength, and that a light's color has a lot to do with its visibility: white lights can be seen farthest away, followed by red, then green. So a relatively small white light may seem to be the same distance off as a larger green that's closer to you.

57

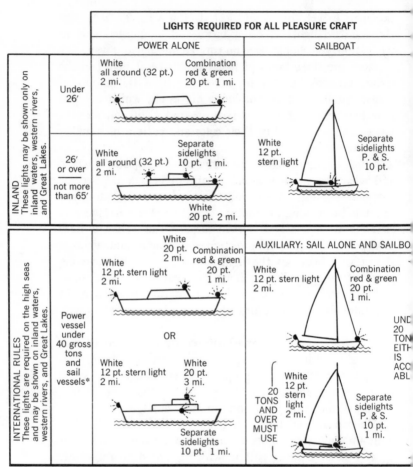

		LIGHTS REQUIRED FOR ALL PLEASURE CRAFT	
		POWER ALONE	SAILBOAT
INLAND These lights may be shown only on inland waters, western rivers, and Great Lakes.	Under 26'	White all around (32 pt.) 2 mi. Combination red & green 20 pt. 1 mi.	
	26' or over not more than 65'	White all around (32 pt.) 2 mi. Separate sidelights 10 pt. 1 mi. White 20 pt. 2 mi.	White 12 pt. stern light Separate sidelights P. & S. 10 pt.
INTERNATIONAL RULES These lights are required on the high seas and may be shown on inland waters, western rivers, and Great Lakes.	Power vessel under 40 gross tons and sail vessels*	White 20 pt. 2 mi. Combination red & green 20 pt. 1 mi. White 12 pt. stern light 2 mi. OR White 12 pt. stern light 2 mi. White 20 pt. 3 mi. Separate sidelights 10 pt. 1 mi.	AUXILIARY: SAIL ALONE AND SAILBO[...] White 12 pt. stern light 2 mi. Combination red & green 20 pt. 1 mi. 20 TONS AND OVER MUST USE White 12 pt. stern light 2 mi. Separate sidelights P. & S. 10 pt. 1 mi. UND[...] 20 TON[...] EITH[...] IS ACC[...] ABL[...]

*Under International Rules powerboats of 40 gross tons must carry separate side-lights, visible 2 miles, and a 20-point white light visible 5 miles. Sailing vessels of 20 gross tons or over must carry separate sidelights, visible 2 miles. Under sail, only boats of less than 20 tons may use a combination lantern. (Note: A vessel under sail alone on the Great Lakes is not required to display a stern light.)

Diagram 19. Lights required on boats under way between sunset and sunrise.

Anchor Lights. Vessels at anchor must display anchor lights except those of not more than 65 feet in length in a "special anchorage area."

Night or day, the key to good position finding is the same:

1. Never lose track of where you are: even if you're out of sight of land, keep a mental note of your course and speed.

2. Never hang your position on a single sight: even if you're nearly positive that the buoy in sight is the one you want, keep looking for a second aid or landmark to confirm the first.

In addition to running lights, you should carry, on a separate switch, an anchor light that shines all around the horizon. A good spotlight, preferably one that doesn't depend on the main boat battery, is also a useful piece of equipment. Use your spotlight sparingly: not only will it temporarily destroy your own night vision, but it can also be a powerful nuisance to others.

5
Compasses and How to Use Them

ALL MAGNETIC compasses are basically the same, consisting of a length of magnetized ferrous metal balanced so that it can swing freely and assume its natural north-south alignment. In a marine compass, the magnetized needle is attached to the bottom of a card on the surface of which is printed a circle divided into equal parts to show the points of compass direction—north, east, south, etc.—and their numerical equivalents based on a maximum of 360 degrees.

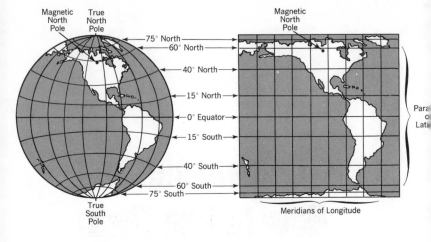

Diagram 20. The round earth and a flat chart.

Map and chart makers have found it handy, in drawing the round earth's surface on a flat piece of paper to superimpose on their maps a reference grid of horizontal and vertical lines, called *parallels of latitude* and *meridians of longitude*, respectively.

While this grid is useful in many ways, it is oriented to the true North Pole, an artificial point at the slightly flattened "top" of the earth. Unfortunately, the magnetic compass doesn't point to true north, but toward the magnetic north pole, the geographical center of the earth's magnetic field, located in far northeastern Canada.

Figure 12. Marine compass indicating magnetic north.

What this means to the user of the marine compass is that he has to make a correction for the difference between magnetic north, which his compass indicates, and true north, the basis of chart grids. On modern charts this correction is printed for you, on a symbolic picture called the compass rose.

The rose is simply a circle divided into 360 equal divisions, called degrees, corresponding to the angular divisions of a circle. By this system, north is 000 degrees, east is 90 degrees, south 180 degrees, and west 270 degrees. (North can also be written 360 degrees, which just brings you back to the beginning.) The north-south line of the rose, indicated by an arrowhead at north, parallels the north-south lines (meridians) on the chart grid.

Inside the larger degree circle is a smaller one, with its north usually cocked off to east or west a few degrees. This circle is magnetic degrees, and the north point is aimed, as your compass points, to magnetic north. A note in the center of the circle tells exactly how many degrees east or west magnetic north is from true—and this angular difference is called variation.

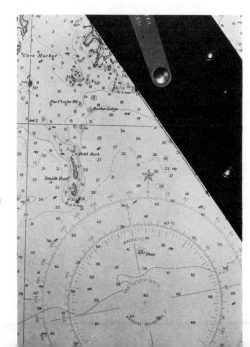

Figure 13. Compass rose within plotting chart.

If you can handle first-year geometry, you can plot a course, because it's practically the same as measuring any other angle. First, draw your course line on the chart (it's best to lay your straightedge between two identifiable points, such as buoys).

Now, using any one of a number of devices called course protractors, construct a line parallel to your course line, running through the center mark of the nearest compass rose. In this case, we've used a very simple gadget called parallel rules, with which a line may be walked (carefully!) from one place to another, always remaining parallel to its original.

Where the second line intersects the outer circle of degree marks on the compass rose is your true course, but to find the course to steer by compass, simply read the degrees from the inner circle.

(You may wonder why charts use true north at all. The reasons are too complex to go into deeply, but they have to do with certain types of compasses which aren't magnetic, and with certain kinds of deep-sea navigation which use true north as a necessary starting point.)

While you're still unsure of your chart and compass work, it's a good idea to practice by laying off short courses between buoys, so you can see the far end of the course leg from the starting point. That way, you'll have a visible check on your compass and a chance to build up your confidence.

Direction is only one part of piloting—the part that tells you *which way*. Equally important is speed/time/distance computation, which reveals *how far* (or *how fast* or *how long*).

There's one simple, basic formula to remember:

$$\text{Distance} = \text{Speed} \times \text{Time}$$

For use on the water, it's modified slightly:

$$\text{Distance} \times 60 = \text{Time in minutes} \times \text{Speed}$$

or
$$60D = ST$$

(which some people remember as an address: "60 D STreet")

A moment's thought will tell you that if the above formula is valid to determine distance, you can twist it around to find time or speed, provided that two of the three elements—*D*, *S* and *T*—are known:

$$60D = ST$$

$$\frac{60D}{S} = T$$

$$\frac{60D}{T} = S$$

For instance: you're going 10 miles an hour, and your objective is 6 miles off. You want to know when you'll arrive:

$$D = 6 \qquad S = 10$$
$$60 \times 6 = 10 \times T, \text{ or 36 minutes}$$

The formula works equally well on inland waters, where land miles of 5,280 feet are used and speeds are expressed in miles per hour, and on coastal waters, where nautical miles of 6,080 feet are the basic distance and speeds are knots (1 knot = 1 nautical mile per hour). Just remember which kind of mile your chart uses.

You'll probably find that when you first try your hand at piloting, you'll make some mistakes. In some cases it will be your own error—not steering properly or working a course or speed wrong. But you may be put wrong by your boat's instruments, especially the compass.

If a compass has a built-in inaccuracy, or if there's a large piece of ferrous metal near the compass mounting, the card may be deflected from magnetic north. This isn't too vital if it's a matter of a degree or two—you can't steer that accurately, anyway. But if your compass is reading 10 or 15 degrees wrong, then it should either be re-sited (placed in a new location) or compensated (corrected by the use of magnets).

Compass compensation is really beyond the scope of this book. If your compass is new and of good quality, it probably has instructions for compensation. If it doesn't have, ask a knowledgeable boating friend (such as a member of the U.S. Coast Guard Auxiliary or U.S. Power Squadrons) for assistance.

There is one other form of error that can creep into your piloting calculations, and that happens when your boat's course is affected by the movement of the water in which it's floating, which is called *current*. A current may be caused by the tide or by a river, and it may help you or hinder you. For small, fast boats, current isn't nearly the factor it is for slow sailing craft, but do remember that if you're heading (for instance) at right angles to a 4-mile-per-hour current for only 15 minutes, you'll be swept sideways a distance of a mile.

Diagram 21. Effect of currents.

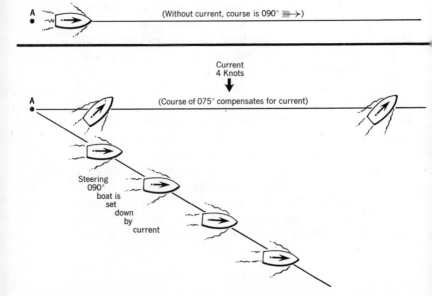

Currents of considerable force are usually indicated on small-craft charts by red arrows with the maximum force of the current printed above.

If you have strong currents—over a couple of miles per hour or knots—in your boating area, learn to take them into account when making a voyage. Mostly this will be by developing a seat-of-the-pants feel for current, by watching its force against pilings or buoys, then noting, against a visible landmark, how your boat is being affected.

As with most small-boat piloting, it's largely a matter of repeated practice and observation.

6

Trailering Your Boat

AS MARINAS and anchorages become more crowded, and as boating continues to spread across the country, more and more people find that trailering their small boat is both a solution to expensive mooring problems and also a good way to cruise previously unreachable waterways. Too, trailering itself has become familiar to more people, thanks to the growing number of house and camp trailers in circulation.

TOWING VEHICLE

The first problem in boat trailering is matching the towing vehicle—usually your family car or station wagon—to the load it must pull: you should consider not only the weight of the boat and trailer, but also the major additional weights of engine, batteries, fuel and gear. Your car dealer can tell you the maximum safe towing load (assuming it's properly supported and hitched) that your car can handle.

69

Figure 14. Load plate.

Assuming you have a boat of less than 8-foot beam, you may trailer her on roads across America without any special permit. Obviously, if your boat is advertised as being trailerable, the manufacturer is saying that her beam is 8 feet or less. Some states impose laws about the maximum combined length of tow plus car (often 50 feet), but this should be no problem. Other state laws (consult your state police for complete details) will have to do with whether or not the trailer must have brakes—all but the very smallest trailers should be so equipped out of common sense if not law—lights, and some type of special connector called a hitch.

TRAILER SUPPORTS

Make sure your trailer supports the boat evenly: boats are designed, after all, to be upheld uniformly at all points below the waterline, and while on a trailer the hull will rest on only a few square inches of its surface. Trailer supports, which are nearly always adjustable, should brace the boat at the transom (for outboard and sterndrive craft) with a wide area of cradle or roller. Inboards should also have some support under the engine bed stringers—the lengthwise framing that supports the engine.

If your boat has a visible keel, the rollers on either side should be adjusted to serve both as supports and as guides.

Figure 15. Support rollers.

Boats without keels should have a guide bar on the back of the trailer to keep the boat centered on the vehicle.

Finally, there should be a bow support, which not only prevents the bow from swaying side to side, but also keeps the boat from running forward over the front of the trailer or dropping back unexpectedly. The bow support of most boats is a pillar on which is mounted a hand or electric winch for working the boat into position. Before buying a winch (which is usually an extra-cost option), make sure that the winch's capacity is the same as the trailer-load rating, and that the winch cable strength is at least 150 percent of the trailer-load capacity.

TRAILER BRAKES

If you require brakes, and they're an option (as they often are), try to get a trailer with electrically or hydraulically operated brakes, which are under the driver's control, instead of so-called "surge" brakes, which are considered dangerous by many authorities because they operate automatically.

TRAILER HITCH

The hitch that connects tow and towing car is a vital joint. Generally it consists of a socket at the forward end of the trailer tongue fitting over a ball mounted on a bracket at the back of the towing vehicle. A lock in the socket keeps the ball from jumping free, and safety chains from trailer to tow hitch hold the trailer on even if the ball and socket fail. Safety chains should always be double, as shown, crossed under the trailer tongue to keep it from dropping and digging into the road at high speed.

Very light loads are often connected to the tow car by a bumper hitch, which fastens directly to the car's bumper. This is inadequate for towing boats and is illegal in some states. For boat-plus-trailer weights up to about 3,500 pounds, a frame hitch, which is welded or bolted to the car's underbody, is the normal arrangement.

Above that trailer weight, the tow car will tend to sag back on its rear springs, and a special weight-distributing hitch is needed. This complex device distributes trailed load to both ends of the towing vehicle, keeping it horizontal.

SECURING LINES

After settling your boat on its trailer so that the hull is evenly supported at all important points, either remove or lash down all loose equipment. There should be a strong, taut line running from the towing eye of the boat to the trailer's winch column, and a nonstretch webbing strap securing the stern to the trailer frame. On larger boats, a pair of spring lines from the bow cleat aft to the rear of the trailer frame will help cushion any surge caused by sudden braking.

TRAILER TONGUE

Now check the weight on the trailer tongue, which should be 5 to 7 percent of the trailer's gross weight. That is, if the boat, plus all her gear aboard, plus the trailer itself weighed 2,000 pounds, then the downward force on the end of the trailer tongue should be between 100 and 140 pounds. You can check this easily enough by propping a bathroom scale on a couple of cinder blocks, then easing down the trailer tongue on the scale platform.

If the weight at the tongue is too much or too little, you can usually move the trailer wheels forward or back on the frame to change the balance. If in doubt, have the trailer dealer do it for you.

SAFETY CHECKS

Before leaving, check brakes, brake lights, wheels and tires. On the road, you should pull off at least every hour to repeat this simple check, which is necessary because trailer wheels, being very small, turn much faster (and consequently wear much more) than your car's wheels.

Also check the main adjustable bolts on the trailer for tightness and all the tie-downs for loosening. Your tools should include a pressure gauge for the trailer's tires, a

Figure 16. Trailer tire-inflation chart.

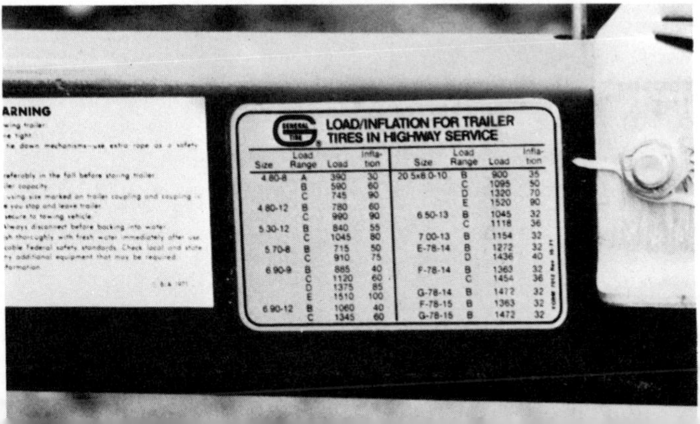

spare trailer tire and wheel, a jack (many car jacks won't fit under a trailer frame), light bulbs for the brake lights, spare grease for wheel bearings, and an extra set of these bearings.

If you're the driver, remember that boat-plus-trailer makes your maneuverable car into a very unwieldy thing which must swing wide for turns, brake early and gently, and allow extra time and distance when overtaking and passing.

Before you attempt an actual launching, it's a good idea to spend an afternoon in a deserted parking lot learning how to back the trailer easily. The accompanying illustrations show the basics of the operation, but only practice will give you the confidence to do the same thing on a steep ramp.

For safety, never back a trailer without having someone stand outside to guide you. If your rig is especially heavy or hard to see around, you may want to fit your car with an auxiliary front bumper hitch, just for launching.

When launching, keep the trailer's hubs out of the water if at all possible, and if you do have to dunk them, then at least let the wheel bearings cool down for 10 minutes or so *before* launching. If bearings get wet, repack them with grease before you drive away. If you don't, you may have to change a burnt-out wheel bearing on the way home.

Never turn the car engine off while launching or recovering, and if you have an automatic transmission, set it in Low with the parking brake on while you wrestle the boat on or off the trailer. If possible, try also to chock the wheels to keep from any possibility of rolling back into the water.

A. Always back with aid of a guide.

B. Try to keep trailer hubs out of the water when launching.

C. Chock car wheels while launching; retain control of bow line.

Figure 17. Launching.

D. As boat slides off trailer, feed out winch line.

E. A helping push may be required at this point.

Figure 17. (Continued)

F. With boat afloat alongside ramp finger pier, check for leaks, necessary equipment, while driver is parking trailer.

BETWEEN TRIPS

At home, shore up the trailer frame between trips to prevent the boat's concentrated weight from bearing down on wheels and springs. The easiest way to do this is with cinder blocks and wood planks, as shown.

If the boat isn't going to be used for some time, the battery should be removed and both vessel and trailer covered with a tarp, loosely tied in place.

7
Boating Emergencies

WHAT MAKES boating emergencies more dangerous, by and large, than the same type of incidents ashore is that you can't run away from a marine accident. Instead, you have to keep your head and cope with the problem. If you have good equipment and the knowledge required to handle it, however, you should be able to deal with nearly any serious emergency on the water.

FIRE

The best way to handle fire afloat is to prevent its ever happening. On smaller boats, the principal danger of fire is in the engine and fuel system, while aboard larger vessels more (if less dangerous) fires arise from mishaps in the galley. If your boat is properly ventilated and you observe normal precautions when fueling, as outlined earlier, your bilge should be free from dangerous fumes.

Still, when coming aboard you should always open the engine compartment hatch (if there is one) and sniff the bilge before starting the engine: fuel-line connections can vibrate or wear through; a sticky carburetor float can cause fuel to keep running after the engine's off. If inspection reveals either vapor or liquid gasoline, get everyone ashore until the boat is thoroughly aired out and the liquid gasoline has been emulsified by adding water and a detergent, then pumped out with a nonsparking pump.

Fire Extinguishers. There are several types of fire extinguishers approved by the Coast Guard for marine use, but far and away the most common is the dry chemical device shown, in which a charge of fine, inert powder is propelled by compressed air to form a smothering cloud. Smaller boats normally carry a single one of these extinguishers, and certain small craft don't have to carry any at all. But only a fool would operate a gasoline-driven boat without a fire extinguisher in good working condition, no matter what the law requires.

Figure 18. Fire extinguisher gauge.

The only problem with dry chemical-type extinguishers is that the powder itself, once released, clogs the extinguisher nozzle in such a way that the extinguisher has to be used all at once: you can't test it with a brief shot, or fire off half and save the rest. A dry chemical extinguisher is strictly a one-time device, to be recharged by your marina or fire department after each use.

Your extinguisher, no matter what the type (see table in Chapter 8), should be inspected and recharged at least once a year, and certainly whenever the pressure gauge shows a low reading.

The extinguisher in its quick-release bracket should be mounted near the helm position in such a way that the man at the wheel can read the gauge easily and break the extinguisher free with a single motion.

If a fire does start, you won't have much time to put it out, especially if it's a gasoline fire: kill the engine immediately, and shut off the fuel supply if you can. Aim the extinguisher at the base of the fire and use it all. If the fire isn't immediately put out and if there are other boats nearby, get your crew and yourself into life preservers and over the side.

Getting Help. Even if you think you've put out the fire, take no chances: get help and have the boat towed home, if the fire was in any way connected with the engine or fuel system. Don't set out again until you discover what caused the fire and correct it.

If no other boats are near and the fire is out of control, get all hands life-jacketed and free of the boat, which will herself make as obvious a distress signal as you'd want.

But in almost every emergency *except* fire, your best bet is to stay with the boat as long as she's even partly afloat. Even a nearly submerged hull is easier for rescuers to see than a couple of heads bobbing in the water, and any sensible skipper will detour to see why a semisunken vessel is awash.

81

COLLISIONS

Collisions between even small boats can be dangerous to the crews involved. If you hit another boat, however lightly, be certain that both vessels are safe before you leave the scene of the accident. The law requires you to do whatever you can to aid the other boat's crew, short of endangering your own passengers and vessel. After a collision, check first to make sure that everyone is still aboard: the first couple of minutes after a crash can be vital to a person who's hurt and in the water. Then check the boat for leaks or other damage: if over $100 of damage has been done, you must file an accident report with the Coast Guard —which you must also do if anyone is killed or injured badly enough to be laid up for 24 hours or more.

If your collision has holed either boat, the other one should stand by and/or try to attract attention while the crippled boat attempts to reach the nearest port. Jam a seat cushion or tarp against the hole from outside and hold it there, but don't beach the boat unless it's absolutely necessary: the surf may end up doing more harm than the collision.

CAPSIZING

Capsizing, or overturning, a seaworthy modern powerboat is almost always the result of overloading—another case in which prevention is nine-tenths of the cure. Should your boat turn over, however, the first thing to do is count heads and make sure no one's trapped under the hull. Have the crew get into life jackets as best they can and collect whatever floating gear is within reach. But don't wear yourselves out for no reason: recent tests have shown that thrashing about in the water quickly uses up energy, leading to exhaustion and exposure.

82

If the boat is afloat, even upside down, stay with her. When rescuers come alongside, get all the crew aboard first, then worry about getting the overturned boat ashore: chances are you're a lot more tired than you realize, and you can always tow the boat in upside down if necessary.

If your swamped boat is upright, you can try to bail her. But if there's any sea at all, this can be a heartbreaking, frustrating thing to do. Concentrate instead on getting help, using one of the several methods for attracting attention when in distress.

DISTRESS SIGNALS

Simplest, if the boat is stable enough for you to stand up, is the arm signal: extend both arms at shoulder height; lift them up till they're near vertical, then lower them to your sides. Do this rhythmically and repeatedly, so observers will understand it's a distress signal and you're not just stretching.

A horn or whistle, blown in repeated short blasts, is another recognized signal of distress, as is any loud noise repeated over and over.

Many skippers carry a flare set, with hand-held red flares for night, orange smoke signals for daytime. Be sure to note the expiration date on all flares, and replace them when they get close to becoming out-of-date.

The same flare kits often carry a distress flag, usually nothing more than a piece of bright red or red-orange plastic. This kind of flag is surprisingly visible at a distance, especially if you have an outrigger, oar or fishing pole to wave it from. In a pinch, the American flag flown upside down is a known signal of distress.

If you spot a distressed boat yourself, you should stand by and help if you can—but not if it means endangering your own vessel and crew. Perhaps you may think it wiser to go for professional help: if so, try to make the distressed skipper realize what you're up to. Make sure also that you can give authorities a good description of the helpless boat and her location.

STORMS

Bad weather seldom arrives without warning, and your first line of defense against it is a good marine weather forecast. But no matter what the professionals say, keep your eyes and wits about you, especially on hazy days. As the white, puffy fair-weather clouds begin to pile up and become darker and more clearly outlined, it may be a sign that a local thunderstorm is building, especially in late afternoon along the coast. Such storms may form in an hour or two, and may carry gusts of 50 miles per hour or even more.

More dangerous is the thunderhead that's hidden by low-lying haze. If you can't see more than a mile, and one part of the sky suddenly begins to darken, you can safely bet it's time to hurry home. If you have an AM radio aboard, the crackling static will frequently warn you of electrical activity in the atmosphere.

And sometimes, in spite of everything, a storm will catch you out. For the small powerboat a squall is dangerous, but cool handling should bring you through. For one thing, a sudden storm is usually over (or at least diminished) in a few minutes, and if you can keep the boat in hand for a quarter to half an hour, the worst should be past.

Head into the wind, throttling back to slow speed—but not so slow you may stall out. Head away from shore or other obstructions; sound fog signals if other boats are nearby. Keep the bilges bailed as dry as you can. If serious waves form, and this usually takes a while even in strong wind, even the smallest shelter—a low island or a reef just under water—can be a very effective barrier between you and the seas.

A narrow harbor entrance, however, can be quite dangerous, especially if the winds and waves are sweeping across its entrance. If you're taking too much of a beating or if you're too low on fuel to stay out, you'll have to try an approach: start from far enough away and upwind so you have a good idea of how much the wind and current are setting you down. Make your pass fairly quickly, just under planing speed for maximum control. Be ready for a confused, directionless chop just off bulkheads or sea walls.

RUNNING AGROUND

Running aground in a small boat is seldom a disaster, unless you puncture the hull. If your boat runs up on a sand- or mudbank, first try backing her off at about half throttle. If she doesn't respond quickly, and if the tide is falling, don't press matters: clouds of sand or mud churned up by the prop can easily get into the cooling system and damage it permanently.

Move whatever weights are loose to the aft end of the boat (assuming you went on bow first). If another powerboat goes past, ask the skipper to throw as big a wake as he can: this will often wash you free. If not, pass him a line. If the other boat isn't big enough to pull you free, ask him to run an anchor out to deep water for you, to keep you from working more firmly aground.

If you have to wait for the next tide, chock your boat's hull with driftwood to keep her from falling over. You can even pass the time by scrubbing the boat's bottom clean.

Before allowing anyone to tow you off, be sure no rocks or coral are between you and deep water. Raise the lower unit out of harm's way. Make your end of the towrope fast to the biggest, sturdiest fitting you have, and ask the other skipper to pull slowly and steadily, not with a series of sharp tugs. Once afloat, check immediately for leaks. Don't let the towboat go till you're sure your own engine will run and the steering gear is undamaged.

8
Checklist for Your New Boat

EQUIPPING A NEW BOAT

THE FOLLOWING list is not gear you *might* be able to use on a new boat; it's deliberately restricted to really necessary or useful equipment for the boat under 26 feet (Classes A and 1).

Item	
Registration: papers and numbers	For all vessels designed to carry engines.
Backfire flame arrester	For all inboard or sterndrive engines (usually installed by builder).
Ventilation	For each engine or fuel storage compartment of a gasoline-powered boat.
Bell	Not required, but necessary to produce proper fog signal at anchor.

Whistle or horn	
Class A:	Not required, but necessary to make proper right-of-way signals.
Class 1:	Required: hand, mouth or power-operated, audible 1 mile.
Personal flotation device	One for each person on or towed by a boat. Life preserver cushions are adequate legally for boats under 16 feet, but better practice is to carry a life vest or jacket for each crewmember.
Anchor	At least 1, with suitable line for local waters (10 times depth of deepest anchorage).
Bilge blower	Desirable for any boat with deep bilge compartment.
Boathook	At least 6 to 8 feet long.
Charts	For local waters.
Compass	Marine type.
Distress signals	Hand-held flares, orange smoke, distress flag.
Dock lines	At least 3, each not less than 25 feet long.
Emergency food and water	For all boats, proportional to crew and normal operating distance offshore.
Fenders	2 to 4.
Fire extinguisher	Although not legally required for certain small outboards, every boat should carry at least 1 and preferably 2 approved B-I size extinguishers.
First-aid kit	Small commercial type for marine use.
Pump	Portable or deck-mounted, depending on type of boat.

Tools and parts   For engine repair; see list in this
                         chapter.

BASIC ENGINE TOOLS FOR THE SMALL BOAT

These are just a beginning. As time goes on, you'll doubt-less accumulate others.

Tool box (plastic tackle box is good).
Engine manual (if you don't have it, write the manu-facturer; also ask for a spare-parts list).
Screwdriver (several, both regular and Phillips head).
Pliers (slip joint; also vise-grip type).
Wrenches (set of open-end or adjustable crescent).
Hammer.
Hacksaw (with extra blades).
File (and sandpaper).
Knife.
Oil can.

Your engine manufacturer may sell a spare-parts kit or may suggest spares to carry. If he doesn't, here are some parts you should know how to install and should carry aboard:

Spark plugs (complete set).
Distributor points.
Spare starter cord (for outboard).
Fuel pump.
Fan belt.
Shear pins.
Coil.
Condenser.
Waterproof electrical tape.
Assorted nuts, bolts and screws.

FLOAT PLAN

Just in case, it's a good idea to have the following information about your boat written down and posted near your home telephone:

Type of boat	Boat name	Boat's home dock
Length	Maximum draft	Registration number
Type of power	Hull color	Flares aboard?
Spotlight?	Topsides color(s)	

Also, it doesn't hurt to jot down the phone numbers of your local Coast Guard, Coast Guard Auxiliary, and marine police units.

MORE BOATING INFORMATION

Two national organizations offer low-cost instruction in boating to the public: the only charge is usually in the neighborhood of $3 to $10 for textbooks and charts used and kept by the student.

U.S. Coast Guard Auxiliary	U.S. Power Squadrons
400 Seventh St., S.W.	Box 345
Washington, D.C. 20591	50 Craig Rd.
	Montvale, N.J. 07645

Write to either address for information about the courses offered and the time and location of the one nearest you.

COURTESY MOTORBOAT EXAMINATION (CME)

A free, voluntary service performed by the civilian members of the Coast Guard Auxiliary (see address above) for owners of pleasure boats. The specially qualified examiner checks your boat for the safety equipment and proper installations noted below. If you pass CME requirements, you receive a decal, to be pasted on your windshield, signifying that this is the case. (As a rule, Coast Guard and marine police safety teams will not board a boat showing this decal.) If you *don't* pass, however, only you are informed: no official report is made to police or Coast Guard.

Safety Equipment and Installations Required for CME Decal:

One approved personal flotation device for each person aboard or each berth, whichever is greater. Minimum of 2.

At least 1 portable fire extinguisher on all Class A and 1 boats, regardless of construction.

Proper navigation lights in working order.

At least 1 distress flare.

Anchor and line.

Oar or paddle, pump or bailer, whistle (Class A boats only).

Backfire flame arrestor, all inboard engines.

Proper ventilation system.

Galley stove (if any) of marine type, properly installed.

Safe fuel and electrical system.

FIRE EXTINGUISHER TYPES

Fire extinguishers are rated in two ways: by their capacity and by the type of fire they're designed to fight. Roughly speaking, Coast Guard-approved fire extinguishers for small boats come in two sizes, small and medium, noted by the roman numerals I and II, respectively. Extinguishers that can deal with fires caused by gasoline, kerosene or grease are rated B; they can also extinguish small electrical fires or burning wood, paper, etc. For small boats, an extinguisher rated B-I or B-II on the label, and containing dry chemical or carbon dioxide, is probably most suitable.

STORM–WARNING SIGNALS

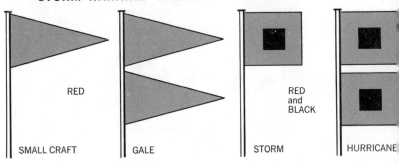

RED

SMALL CRAFT

GALE

RED
and
BLACK

STORM

HURRICANE

Diagram 22. Storm warnings.

The illustration above shows the various signals—flags by day, red-and-white lights at night—which may be hoisted at official weather-warning stations. Any one of these signals indicates coming weather that could be dangerous for a small open boat—you're well advised to stay in port.

CONCLUSION

Much of this book has dealt with possible accidents, bad weather, and other rough going. It may seem that boating is all disaster—which is absolutely not the case at all. Most skippers pass their entire boating careers without ever being involved in a serious accident; many boatmen go years between even minor difficulties on the water. By and large, these people aren't so much lucky as they are forearmed—they know how to avoid getting into trouble.

That's what this book is intended partly to do: the fun of boating you can discover yourself, and you will discover it more certainly if you know what to look out for and if you learn the rudiments of boating presented here. With these principles firmly lodged in the back of your mind, so that following them is second nature, you'll be able to concentrate on enjoying yourself afloat, which is what boating is really all about.